The Immune System

Injury, Illness and Health

Carol Ballard

Heinemann
LIBRARY

www.heinemann.co.uk/library
Visit our website to find out more information about **Heinemann Library** books.

To order:
☎ Phone 44 (0) 1865 888066
🖹 Send a fax to 44 (0) 1865 314091
💻 Visit the Heinemann Bookshop at www.heinemann.co.uk/library to browse our catalogue and order online.

First published in Great Britain by Heinemann Library,
Halley Court, Jordan Hill, Oxford
OX2 8EJ, part of Harcourt Education.

Heinemann is a registered trademark of Harcourt Education Ltd.

Editorial: Sarah Eason and Georga Godwin
Design: Jo Hinton-Malivoire and AMR
Illustrations: Art Construction
Picture Research: Rosie Garai and Debra Weatherley
Production: Viv Hichens

Originated by Blenheim Colour Ltd
Printed in Hong Kong, China
by Wing King Tong

ISBN 0 431 15705 7
07 06 05 04 03
10 9 8 7 6 5 4 3 2 1

British Library Cataloguing in Publication Data
Ballard, Carol
The Immune System. – (Body Focus)
616'.079
A full catalogue record for this book is available from
the British Library.

Acknowledgements
The Publishers would like to thank the following for
permission to reproduce photographs: Alamy p. **43**;
Arena/PAL p. **35**; Corbis p. **41**; Corbis/Bettman p. **36**;
Cornell University p. **37**; NHPA/Anthony Bannister p.
6; SPL/Aaron Haupt p. **27**; SPL/Alfred Pasieka p. **21**;
SPL/CNRI pp. **34**, **42**; SPL/Cordelia Molloy p. **32**;
SPL/Dr Andrejs Liepjns pp. **22 (left)**, **22 (right)**;
SPL/Dr Kari Lounatnaa p. **15**; SPL/Dr P. Marazzi pp.
7, **13**; SPL/Ed Young p. **40**; SPL/James Holmes,
Celltec Ltd p. **29**; SPL/James King Holmes p. **33**;
SPL/Mark Clarke p. **18**; SPL/Matt Meadows, Peter
Arnold Inc p. **9**; SPL/National Library of Medicine p.
26; SPL/Professor S. Cinti/CNRI p. **30**; SPL/Science
Pictures Ltd p. **8**; SPL/Scott Camazine/ CDCDC p. **38**;
SPL/Secchj Loecadle/ CNRI p. **20**; SPL/Susumu
Nishimaga p. **10**.

The cover image of a Transmission Electron
Micrograph of the AIDS virus appears courtesy of
Science Photo Library/Chris Bjonberg.

The Publishers would like to thank David Wright for
his assistance with the preparation of this book.

CONTENTS

Words appearing in the text in bold, **like this**, are explained in the Glossary.

INTRODUCTION

Your immune system is your body's defence mechanism against disease. It involves a variety of cells, tissues and organs, all of which work together in different ways to keep your body free from illness and disease. Some mechanisms are non-specific, responding in the same way to any potential problem. Other mechanisms are very specific, responding only to a single stimulus.

Skin

Your body is completely covered by skin, which provides your body's first means of defence. It forms a barrier between your tissues and the air around you, preventing dirt and **microbes** from entering your body.

Blood

Your blood plays an important part in defending your body. It is an efficient transport system, carrying essential chemicals and cells to sites of injury, and removing dead cells and other debris. **Platelets** help to form scabs over wounds, keeping infection out and allowing healing to take place. White blood cells act in a variety of ways to prevent infections and diseases.

Lymphatic system

Your lymphatic system is a network of drainage tubes and associated tissues and organs. A watery fluid, called **lymph**, flows around your body through this network. White blood cells are produced in the red **bone marrow**, and some travel to lymphoid tissue to mature. Many white blood cells are stored in **lymph nodes**, to be released into the bloodstream when they are needed. Some microbes can be trapped in lymph nodes, for destruction by white blood cells.

Doctors use methods such as vaccination to stimulate the immune system and prevent disease.

This diagram shows the lymphatic system, the network of channels through which lymph flows around your body. The lymph nodes, **spleen** and **thymus** are also part of the system.

Blood cells play an important part in defending your body. Different blood cells respond in different ways. Your skin provides an effective barrier, stopping microbes from entering your body.

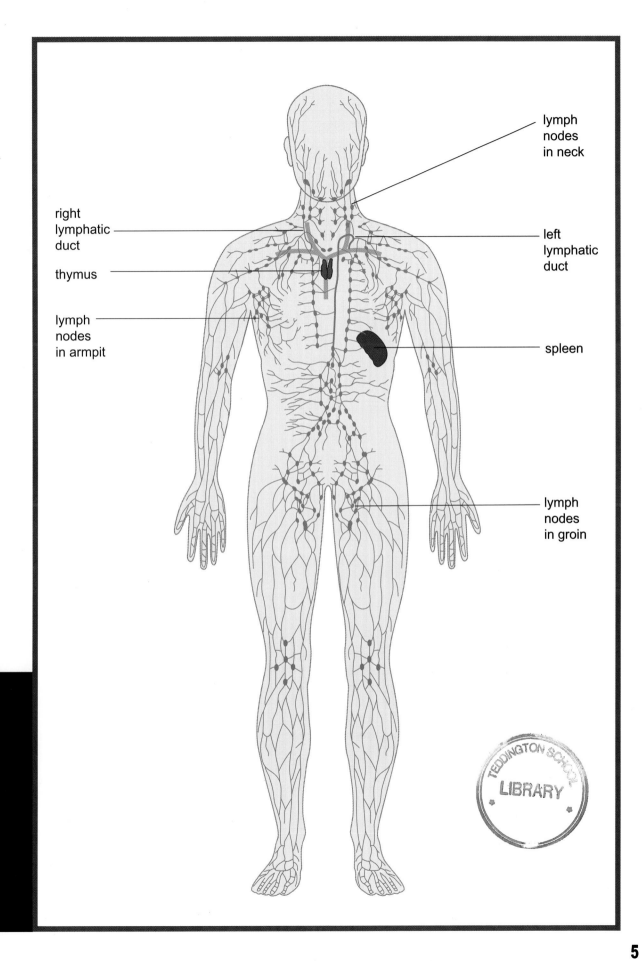

lymph
nodes
in neck

right
lymphatic
duct

left
lymphatic
duct

thymus

lymph
nodes
in armpit

spleen

lymph
nodes
in groin

5

DEFENCE AGAINST WHAT?

Your body is exposed to many different chemicals, foreign materials and **microbes** every day of your life. The majority do not pose any threat at all, but some could cause damage and illness. Your body must defend itself against these. It must also recognize and defend itself against any abnormal changes that occur within it.

Foreign objects

The inside of your body needs to be kept as clean as possible and so it is important that dust, dirt and other foreign objects are prevented from entering it.

Toxins

Toxins are poisonous chemicals made by other animals, plants or **micro-organisms**. Some cause only a small reaction, such as a rash after touching a stinging nettle, or a sore red area after an insect bite. Your body can successfully defend itself against such toxins, and little damage occurs. Some toxins, such as those found in snake venom, are much more dangerous and can be deadly, because your body has no adequate defence against them.

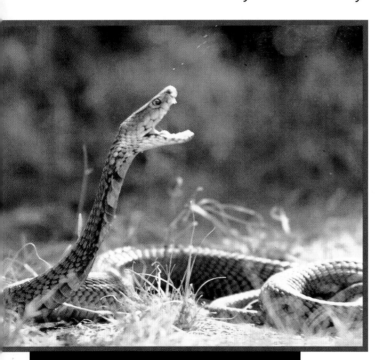

Your body has mechanisms to defend itself against toxins. Some, such as that found in this snake's venom, are just too powerful and can be deadly.

Chemicals and poisons

Many everyday chemicals, such as bleach and weedkiller, are potentially dangerous if misused. Your body can defend itself against some, but not all. Your best protection is to make sure that you do not expose yourself to any chemicals unnecessarily, and always to carefully follow the instructions.

Bacteria

These are very small micro-organisms, less than 0.001 millimetre long. There are many different types of **bacteria**. Some are entirely harmless and some, such as the bacteria found in the large intestine, are actively useful. However, some bacteria can cause serious illnesses, such as *Escherichia coli* (*E. coli*) that causes serious food poisoning, and *Mycobacterium tuberculosis*, which causes tuberculosis (TB), a lung disease.

Bacterial infections can occur by eating infected food, inhaling bacteria, contact with another infected person and by exposure of a wound to bacteria in the air.

Viruses

Viruses are much smaller than bacteria and can pass through filters that bacteria cannot. They are transmitted in the same ways as bacteria, and cause many common diseases, such as influenza (flu), chickenpox and the common cold.

Parasites

Some organisms are parasitic – they live inside a host body and derive their nourishment from it. Some may eventually kill their host. Some parasites, such as tapeworms, can enter the body via our food, particularly when we eat meat that is not fully cooked. Others, such as the plasmodium that causes malaria, may be passed to humans by mosquitoes.

Athlete's foot is caused by a fungus growing on the dead skin of the feet.

Abnormal body tissues

Your body is made up of trillions and trillions of cells. These continuously grow, divide, die and are replaced by new cells. For the majority of the time, this cycle continues perfectly. Very, very occasionally, a change may occur in a cell or group of cells that makes it grow or divide more rapidly than usual. These changes can lead to the growth of a tumour. If your body recognizes these changes, it can stop the tumour developing by destroying the abnormal cells.

Fungi

These microbes are very important to humans – yeast makes bread rise, and also ferments alcohol to make wine and beer, and mushrooms are ingredients used in many recipes around the world. However, some fungi can cause diseases. Athlete's foot is an infection caused by a fungus, called *Trichophyton*, which lives and grows on the dead skin of the feet. Ringworm is caused by a different fungus, *Microsporum*, that grows in a ring (usually on the head), causing red, itchy patches. Fungal infections are generally passed from person to person by direct contact, or by contact with contaminated items, such as towels.

Many infections can easily be spread from one person to another. It makes sense to take precautions against picking up infections yourself, and also to avoid passing them on to others.

Keeping skin, hair, teeth and nails clean should be a natural part of everybody's daily routine. It prevents a buildup of **microbes**, and reduces the chances of infections.

Spots

Spots can be a real nuisance, especially when you are a teenager. They often occur as a result of the overproduction of oil by the skin. The excess oil blocks the pores, and **bacteria** build up and feed off the oil. Washing the skin regularly helps to remove the excess oil and the bacteria. Some people find cleansing lotions useful and, in severe cases, doctors may prescribe **antibiotic** creams.

Clean hands

Our hands are in contact with many things every day. As a result, dirt and microbes collect on the skin. It is important to wash your hands thoroughly before you prepare food, to avoid contaminating the food. The places where food is stored and prepared also need to be kept clean, along with any utensils used. Before you eat, you should wash your hands to avoid dirt or microbes being taken in with the food.

It is very important that you wash your hands after using the toilet. Human waste is full of microbes, and these can easily be transferred onto your hands. Washing removes the microbes, preventing contamination of other surfaces, and reducing the risk of your making yourself and others ill.

The bacteria growing in this dish came from a person's unwashed hands.

Coughing and sneezing

Viruses, such as those that cause the common cold and influenza (flu), can be passed from one person to another by 'droplet infection'. When you cough or sneeze, droplets of moisture containing virus particles are forced out of your mouth and nose into the air around you. Sneezing into a handkerchief, and putting a hand in front of your mouth when you cough, ensures that the droplets are trapped and disposed of, and not left suspended in the air for someone else to breath in.

When you sneeze, droplets of moisture are forced out of your nose into the air.

Spitting

Although most people are probably familiar with the image of footballers spitting on the pitch to clear their mouths, spitting excess saliva out of the mouth is less common now than it used to be. It really is something you should try never to do, because germs are easily spread in this way.

Some of the things that your body needs to defend itself against are quite general. Your body does not need to recognize exactly what it is protecting itself from; it just needs to mount a simple defence. There are several efficient mechanisms for doing this.

The air that you breathe in contains dust, dirt and **microbes**. Ideally, these all need to be prevented from entering your lungs. The inside surfaces of your nose and windpipe are covered with a **membrane** that produces sticky **mucus**. The tiny particles get trapped in the mucus. Fine hairs sweep the mucus away from the lungs, keeping them clean and free from dirt.

Eye protection

Dust and dirt can make your eyes itchy and damage the delicate surfaces. Eyelashes act as filters, keeping many particles away from the surfaces of the eyes. Tears wash over the eyes to clean them. Tears also contain an **enzyme**, called lysozyme, which destroys **bacteria**.

Saliva in your mouth washes over your teeth to clean them. It also prevents microbes from growing inside your mouth.

This photograph is a coloured scan from an electron micrograph showing the tiny hairs of the nose.

Stomach

Your stomach can usually deal effectively with any microbes that enter it. The digestive juices inside your stomach are extremely acidic, and will kill most microbes. If toxins enter the stomach, you may vomit to expel them from your body. Toxins and microbes that get past your stomach defences travel on through your digestive system. If they irritate the lining of your **intestines**, the muscles in the intestinal walls contract strongly. You then suffer from diarrhoea as the microbes are rapidly expelled from your body, along with normal digestive waste.

Sebum

Your skin forms a barrier between your body tissues and the air around you. Glands in the skin produce an oily substance, called sebum, which forms a protective film on top of the skin. Sebum can prevent some bacteria and fungi from growing. The skin is also slightly acidic, and this, too, helps to prevent microbe growth. Sweat helps to wash microbes from the skin, and it also contains lysozyme, the same enzyme that is found in tears.

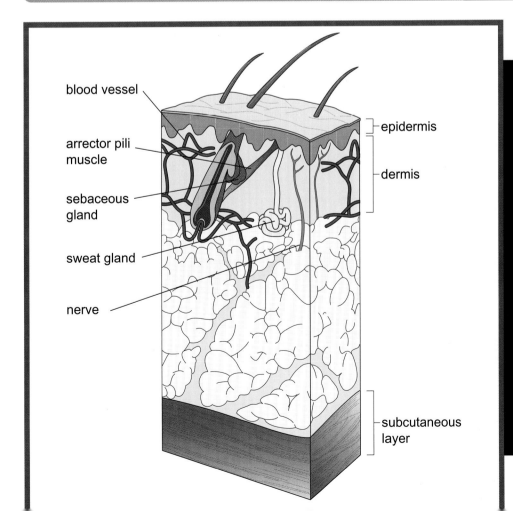

blood vessel

arrector pili muscle

sebaceous gland

sweat gland

nerve

epidermis

dermis

subcutaneous layer

This diagram shows the structure of the skin, your body's natural barrier. The sweat glands produce sweat and the sebaceous glands produce sebum. Both sweat and sebum help to prevent the growth of microbes.

INFLAMMATORY RESPONSE

Damage to body tissues usually results in an '**inflammatory response**'. This is non-specific – your body will react in the same way, whatever the cause of the damage. The skin becomes red and hot, and there is usually swelling and pain.

Causes

Inflammation can be caused by infection by either a **virus** or **bacteria**, by a physical injury, such as a cut, burn, or bruise or by an allergic reaction. Whatever the cause, the process of inflammation is the same. However, the speed of response may be different – some responses occur within seconds, others develop slowly over several days.

Steps in the inflammation process

1. Chemical release: when tissue is damaged, a range of different chemicals, including **histamine**, are released. Some of these chemicals affect the local blood vessels; some attract **phagocytes** (blood cells that engulf foreign material) to the area and some begin the clotting process to seal the damaged area.

These diagrams show the sequence of events in an inflammatory response:

1. Chemicals are released.
2. Blood vessels widen and their walls become more permeable.
3. Phagocytes arrive.
4. Healing begins.

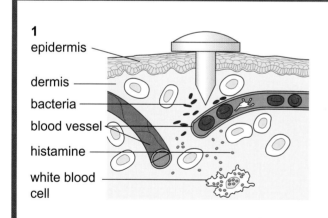

1
- epidermis
- dermis
- bacteria
- blood vessel
- histamine
- white blood cell

2 swelling

injured cell

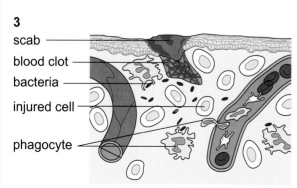

3
- scab
- blood clot
- bacteria
- injured cell
- phagocyte

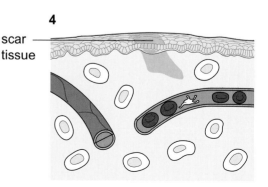

4
- scar tissue

2. Increased blood flow: blood vessels in the damaged area respond to the chemicals released by widening, so that more blood can flow through them, speeding up the removal of toxins and dead cells. At the same time, the walls of the blood vessels become more permeable, allowing chemicals and specialized blood cells to pass through them into the tissues.

The increased blood flow causes the tissues to become hot and red, and may lead to swelling. Pain can be due to damage to nerve fibres, irritation by toxins or by pressure from the swelling.

3. Arrival of phagocytes: phagocytes move out of the bloodstream, through the blood vessel walls and into the damaged tissues. They engulf and destroy damaged tissue, worn out blood cells and **microbes**.

4. Healing: when all the damaged tissue and microbes have been removed, new tissue can begin to grow back into the damaged area. As this healing begins, the phagocytes die and collect together with other debris to form a liquid called pus. This may drain away internally or seep out through the skin. If pus cannot drain away, an abscess may form.

In this photograph, you can see the red, swollen area of inflammation from a wasp sting. It will probably also feel hot and painful.

Abscesses

Most abscesses are minor and cause little problem, but others can be more severe and potentially dangerous. The bacterial infection and pus usually cause an area of redness that is hot, swollen and painful. **Lymph nodes** close to the site of the abscess may also swell as the immune system fights the infection. Some abscesses clear up on their own, but others may be treated with **antibiotics** to kill the bacteria. If there is a lot of pus, it may be necessary for a doctor to make a small cut in the skin to allow it to drain away. The main danger with an abscess is that it may release harmful bacteria into the bloodstream, and the infection may spread through the body.

PHAGOCYTOSIS

Phagocytosis is the process by which a cell surrounds, engulfs and destroys other cells, **microbes** and debris. It is carried out by specialized white blood cells called **neutrophils** and **macrophages**.

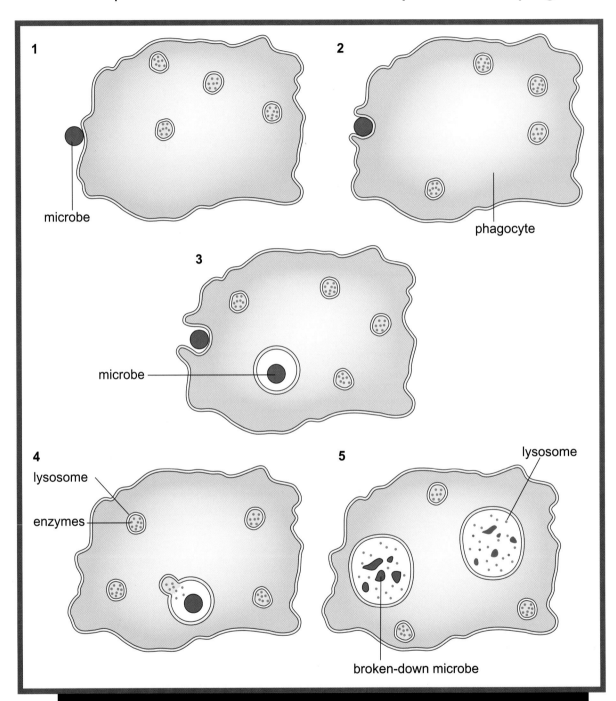

These diagrams show how a microbe is destroyed by phagocytosis:

1. A phagocyte is attracted to an area of damage by chemicals.
2. The phagocyte attaches itself to a microbe.
3. The phagocyte surrounds and engulfs the microbe.
4. Enzymes from a lysosome break down the microbe.
5. The chemicals from the microbe are emptied outside the phagocyte.

There are five main stages in the process of phagocytosis:

1. Chemical attraction – 'chemotaxis': phagocytes are attracted to an area of damaged tissue by special chemicals that are released by other white blood cells, damaged tissue cells and some microbes.

2. Attachment – 'adherence': the phagocyte attaches itself to the surface of a microbe.

3. Engulfing – 'ingestion': the cell membrane of the phagocyte slowly surrounds the microbe, engulfing it completely. The microbe is sealed inside a small sac of the phagocyte's membrane. This detaches itself from the rest of the membrane and moves further into the phagocyte.

4. Breakdown – 'digestion': the sac containing the microbe fuses with a bag-like structure called a lysosome. This contains enzymes that break down every part of the microbe into separate chemicals.

5. Expulsion – 'exocytosis': some of the chemicals released by the breakdown of the microbe may be used by the phagocyte. Any unwanted chemicals are emptied away outside the phagocyte.

In this photograph, taken with an electron micrograph, you can see bacteria that have been engulfed by two phagocytes.

bacteria

blue: phagocytes

LYMPHATIC SYSTEM

The lymphatic system consists of a network of drainage tubes: lymphatic vessels, **lymph nodes**, the **spleen** and the **thymus**. **Lymph** flows around the body through the lymphatic vessels, removing excess fluid and white blood cells from body tissues.

The spleen

The spleen is about 12 centimetres long, and lies between the ribs and the stomach on the left side of the body. It has a rich supply of blood vessels and lymphatic vessels, and plays an important part in filtering the blood. The spleen is also a storage site for blood, releasing it to the body as needed. An outer capsule encloses two types of tissue, red pulp and white pulp. Red pulp consists of veins and spaces around them, both filled with blood. White pulp is lymphatic tissue, mainly white blood cells arranged around central arteries.

As the spleen filters the blood, dead and abnormal blood cells are removed and recycled. It also removes **microbes** and toxins and, as the white blood cells within the spleen come into contact with them, a specific immune response may begin.

Abdominal injury can rupture the spleen. If this happens, the spleen must be removed rapidly, to prevent massive internal bleeding. In some illnesses, the spleen may become enlarged and may need to be removed. Although the spleen is important, patients can live quite normally without it, because the red **bone marrow** and liver can take over its functions.

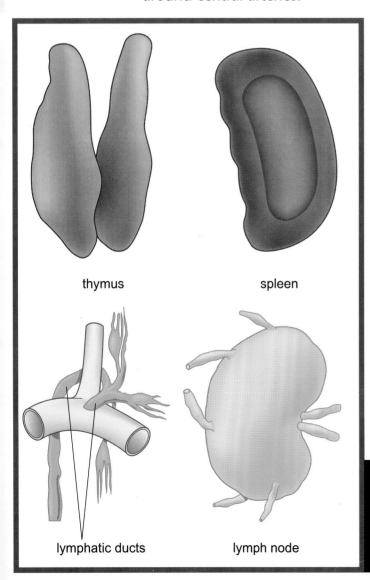

thymus   spleen

lymphatic ducts   lymph node

These diagrams show the thymus, spleen, lymphatic ducts and a lymph node.

The thymus

The thymus gland is a mass of lymphoid tissue in the chest, above the heart. It has two lobes, joined by connective tissue and surrounded by an outer capsule. Each lobe has two areas, the cortex and the medulla. The thymus gland is small, weighing only 12–15 grams at birth. It enlarges during childhood to reach a maximum size of about 35 grams in the early teens. It then slowly shrinks, and may only weigh 3 grams in old age. It is most active during childhood, when it is involved in the development of specific immune responses. Some white blood cells travel to the thymus to mature and develop.

Tonsils

The tonsils are small lymphatic nodules inside a capsule. There are three pairs, one pair at the base of the tongue, one pair split at each side of the soft palate (the partition between the nose and mouth) and one pair behind the nose (often called the adenoids). Together, they form a chain of lymphoid tissue at the entrances to the throat, to prevent infections reaching the lungs and digestive system. They contain white blood cells, to destroy invading microbes.

The tonsils themselves often become infected and may be removed by doctors. This is a minor procedure, and the patient usually suffers no side effects.

This is a cross-section of a lymph node.

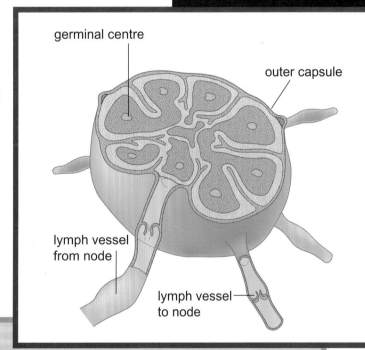

germinal centre

outer capsule

lymph vessel from node

lymph vessel to node

Lymph nodes

These are small, bean-like swellings along the lymphatic vessels. They are spread throughout the body, but there are large numbers of them in the armpits, groin and neck. They have an outer capsule, with finger-like branches of tissue inside that divide them into separate spaces (rather like segments in an orange). At the heart of each segment is the germinal centre, where some white blood cells are produced.

Lymph nodes store white blood cells, releasing them when they are needed into the lymphatic vessels, from where they can move into the bloodstream. Lymph nodes also trap microbes for destruction by the white blood cells.

SPECIFIC IMMUNITY

In addition to general forms of defence, your body can mount a range of highly effective responses against specific **microbes** and other invading agents. Such a response is specific to that stimulus alone, and will not offer any protection against a different stimulus.

Specific immunity is the name given to the body's response to a specific stimulus. A stimulus that makes the body respond is called an **antigen**. There are two important differences between specific immunity and general defence mechanisms:

- Specific immunity protects against one antigen only, whereas general defence mechanisms protect the body from a whole range of invading agents.
- Specific immunity involves a memory function, so that a second exposure to the antigen leads to a very strong and rapid response, while general defence mechanisms do not involve a memory function.

Specific immunity may be innate or acquired.

Innate immunity

Innate immunity means immunity that you are born with. Some species are immune to diseases that affect other species, for example, humans are immune to canine distemper, which affects dogs. Within a species, some individuals are immune to diseases that affect other individuals. If one child in a family catches chickenpox, for example, a brother or sister may be exposed to the **virus** but not develop the disease.

This child has chickenpox – but catching it when he is young allows his body to defend itself against chickenpox for the rest of his life.

Acquired immunity

Any immunity that you are not born with must have been acquired at some time in your life by exposure to a specific antigen. The body responds to the antigen, and is then able to store the memory of the antigen.

There are several ways of acquiring immunity:

Active immunity:
- Immunity can be acquired by natural exposure to the antigen during the course of a disease. This can provide lifelong immunity – having chickenpox as a child, for example, means that you are extremely unlikely to suffer from it a second time.
- Immunity can also be acquired by artificial exposure to the antigen. This can be achieved by injection of dead or weakened antigens in vaccines. These stimulate the body to mount a specific immune response. They can provide lifelong protection, but some, such as tetanus, require repeated injections (boosters) every few years.

Passive immunity:
- Immunity can be acquired naturally from outside the body. Immunity can pass from a mother to her baby during pregnancy or breastfeeding. This provides protection for several months, while the baby's own immune system is developing.
- Immunity can be acquired by injecting serum from an immune person into another individual. This provides protection for a short period of weeks or months.

Exercise and immunity

Research has shown that there may be a link between exercise and immunity. Scientists think that light to moderate exercise can boost the immune system, but that high-intensity exercise can actually have a negative effect on your health. Try not to train too hard when there is a high risk of infection – such as in the winter, when there are lots of coughs and colds about. It is also a good idea to reduce the intensity of exercises when you are under extra physical or emotional stress.

This table summarizes the different ways of acquiring immunity.

Aquired immunity	Active	Passive
natural	exposure to antigen during the course of a disease	from mother to baby during pregnancy or breastfeeding
artificial	injection of dead or weakened antigen	injection of immune serum

WHITE BLOOD CELLS

The body's defences against invading **microbes** and abnormal cells are carried out by white blood cells. There are several different types of white blood cells, each specialized to carry out its own specific function. Together, white blood cells are known as 'leukocytes'.

All white blood cells originate from **stem cells** in the red **bone marrow**. As these divide, further cells are produced, and these, in turn, divide to produce even more cells. The process is like a cascade, with subtle changes taking place at each stage so that, from one original stem cell, a whole range of highly specialized cells are produced.

The origination of white blood cells:

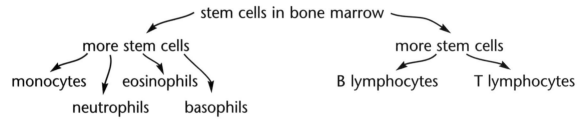

stem cells in bone marrow

more stem cells → monocytes, neutrophils, eosinophils, basophils

more stem cells → B lymphocytes, T lymphocytes

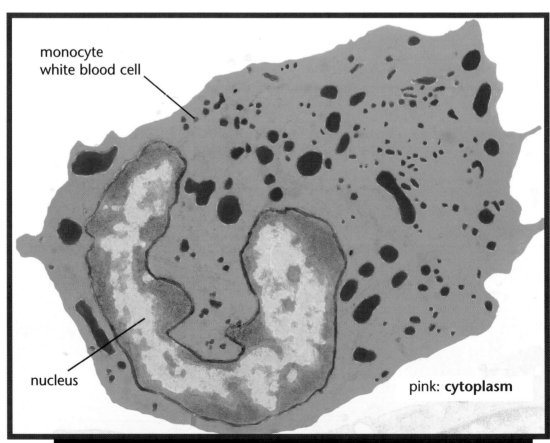

monocyte white blood cell

nucleus

pink: **cytoplasm**

This photograph has been taken using a microscope. The white blood cell has been stained with chemicals so that the internal structures can be seen.

Types of white blood cell

Cells from stem cells are produced in the bone marrow. Some are fully matured when they leave. **Neutrophils** are specialized **phagocytes**, involved in general defence mechanisms, engulfing and destroying microbes and other cells. Monocytes are types of phagocytes, too – they move into body tissues and enlarge to become wandering **macrophages**. These also engulf and destroy microbes and dead tissue cells. Eosinophils and basophils are involved in **allergic reactions** and **inflammatory responses**.

This photograph is of red marrow inside a bone. It is from this tissue that white blood cells develop.

Lymphocytes

Some cells from stem cells leave the bone marrow before they are fully mature. These cells develop into **lymphocytes** at other places in the body. There are two main groups of lymphocytes:

- B lymphocytes: leave the bone marrow and travel to lymphoid tissues, such as the **spleen** and **lymph nodes**. They colonize the lymphoid tissue, and more B lymphocytes are produced in these tissues, without the involvement of the bone marrow. B lymphocytes are involved in specific immune responses, producing chemical responses to specific **antigens**.

- T lymphocytes: also leave the bone marrow, and travel straight to the **thymus**, where they develop fully. They are involved in specific immune responses, regulating the actions of B lymphocytes and other cells. Some T lymphocytes can kill microbes and other cells.

CELL-MEDIATED IMMUNITY

The body's response to a specific **antigen** consists of several different processes and pathways. These are interlinked, but can be thought of in two main categories: responses by specific cells (cell-mediated immunity), and responses involving the release of chemicals called **antibodies**. Many antigens provoke both types of response.

T-cells

T **lymphocytes** (T-cells) are responsible for cell-mediated immunity. Their responses involve direct contact between the T-cell and the antigen, and they always involve attacking and killing cells. Cell-mediated responses occur when T-cells are stimulated by parasites, fungi, **bacteria** and **viruses**. They also occur when T-cells recognize abnormal body cells, such as cancer cells and tissue transplant cells.

There are three main types of T-cell:

- Helper T-cells: these help to activate B lymphocytes and macrophages. They also help other T-cells.
- Suppressor T-cells: these suppress the responses of other cells, preventing the immune system from overreacting and damaging the body itself.
- Killer T-cells: these have specific receptors for antigens. When they come into direct contact with a **microbe** or other abnormal cell, they release chemicals onto its surface that make the target cell leaky, which destroys it.

The top electron micrograph shows a large cancer cell and a smaller killer T-cell. In the bottom picture, you can see that the cancer cell is beginning to leak as chemicals from the T-cells attack its **membrane**.

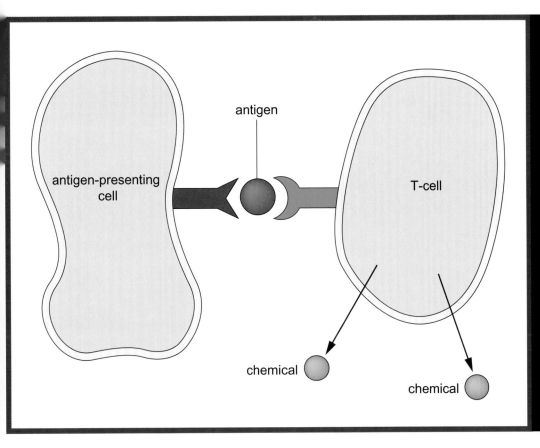

antigen

antigen-presenting cell

T-cell

chemical

chemical

In cell-mediated immunity, an antigen is picked up by an antigen-presenting cell, and displayed for a T-cell to identify as foreign and attack. The T-cell then produces chemicals that alert other cells in the immune system that there is an infection.

Balancing act

The helper cells and suppressor cells have a finely tuned control over the system, balancing each other and making sure that exactly the right level of immune response is generated.

There are millions of different T-cells, each programmed to respond to one specific antigen. When a T-cell meets the antigen it is programmed to recognize, it divides over and over to produce a clone of identical T-cells, all programmed to recognize the antigen. Some of these become helper cells, some become suppressor cells and others become killer cells. The killer cells kill the cells carrying the antigen. Once all the cells are killed, the suppressor cells take over and the immune response fades away. Any T-cells from the clone that are left become 'memory cells'. If the same antigen invades the body again, thousands of memory cells are ready to mount an immediate response. At this point, there are more memory cells and the response is much faster and stronger than it was the first time the antigen was encountered.

Cancer cells

Cancer cells have special antigens on their surfaces that are not on the surfaces of normal cells. Some T-cells are programmed to recognize these antigens and to destroy the cells swiftly, preventing a tumour from growing and developing.

B **lymphocytes** respond to **antigens** by releasing chemicals called **antibodies**, which circulate in the **lymph** and blood. Each antibody is specific to one particular antigen, and the antibody and antigen become attached to each other when they meet.

There are millions of different B lymphocytes (B-cells), each programmed to respond to one specific antigen by producing and releasing one specific type of antibody.

A B-cell will become activated when it comes into contact with the antigen it is programmed to respond to. It divides again and again, producing a clone of identical B-cells. Each cell produces identical antibody molecules, and releases them into the blood and lymph.

This diagram shows how antibodies and antigens 'fit' together, making it easier for phagocytes to destroy the antigen.

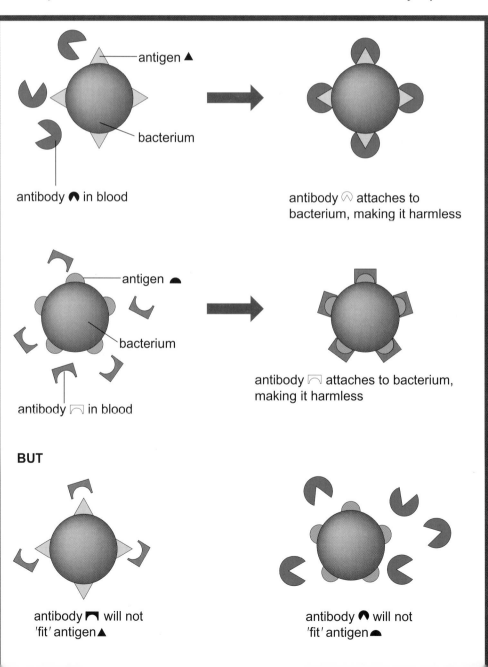

antigen ▲

bacterium

antibody ⌒ in blood

antibody ⌒ attaches to bacterium, making it harmless

antigen ◖

bacterium

antibody ⌒ in blood

antibody ⌒ attaches to bacterium, making it harmless

BUT

antibody ⌒ will not 'fit' antigen ▲

antibody ⌒ will not 'fit' antigen ◖

When antibody and antigen combine

Each antibody molecule can combine with the specific antigen – they fit together rather like a lock and key. The main effect of their combining is to make it easier for **phagocytes** to engulf and destroy the antigen.
Other things can also happen when the antigen and antibody combine, including:

* some bacterial toxins are neutralized so they cannot do any further damage
* some **viruses** are made harmless by being prevented from attaching to body cells
* some **bacteria** are prevented from moving
* some **microbes** are forced to clump together.

Unlike T-cells, the B-cells stay in their place in the lymphoid tissue. All that circulate are the antibody molecules. When the response is over, any B-cells from the clone that remain become 'memory cells', able to mount a swift and strong response if the body is exposed to that same antigen again.

These diagrams show how the protein chains are arranged in the different types of Ig molecule.

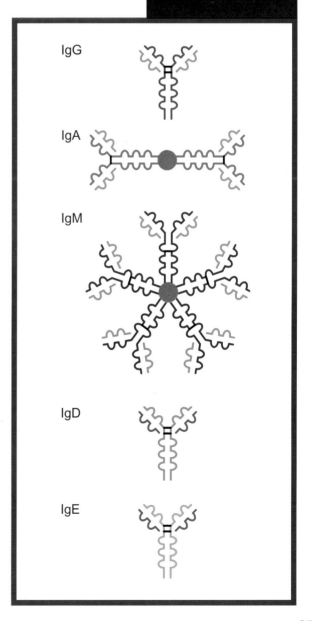

IgG

IgA

IgM

IgD

IgE

What are antibodies?

Antibodies are complex **protein** molecules, called immunoglobulins (Ig). There are five main types: IgA, IgD, IgE, IgG and IgM. Each molecule is made up of protein chains, both heavy and light. The chains are arranged differently in different types of Ig molecule. Some parts of the chains are constant and are the same for all the Ig molecules. Other parts of the chains are variable, allowing each Ig molecule to be specific for one specific antigen.

Vaccination is a way of providing protection against potentially dangerous diseases by exposing the immune system to a small amount of disease material that has been made harmless. Massive vaccination programmes around the world have led to many diseases becoming almost eliminated. However, there are still arguments about how safe some vaccinations are.

The first vaccination

The first recorded vaccination was carried out by Dr Edward Jenner in England in 1796. At that time, smallpox was a deadly disease, which killed many people every year. Cowpox was a similar disease that affected cows. Humans could catch cowpox, too, but it was much less serious than smallpox. Jenner noticed that milkmaids who caught cowpox did not catch smallpox.

Jenner decided to try an experiment. He infected a young boy with cowpox and waited for him to fully recover. Then, Jenner infected the boy with the deadly smallpox, and waited to see what would happen. He hoped that the previous exposure to cowpox would protect the boy and save him from developing smallpox. Jenner was right. The boy stayed well.

Other doctors and scientists were not convinced at first. Jenner carried out more experiments and published his results. His process became known as vaccination, taken from the Latin word for a cow – 'vacca'. Eventually, Jenner's ideas became accepted, and vaccination became widespread. Vaccination against smallpox has been very successful and, today, smallpox is found only in freezers in secure biological laboratories.

Edward Jenner developed the technique of vaccination against smallpox.

Developing vaccines

Following Jenner's work on smallpox, scientists began to develop vaccines for other diseases. The most well-known of these are Louis Pasteur's vaccine for rabies, discovered in the 1880s, and Jonas Salk's vaccine for poliomyelitis, which came into general use in the early 1950s.

This child is being vaccinated to protect her from serious childhood diseases.

Vaccination programmes

Most countries now run comprehensive vaccination programmes, which start when children are very young. Many people are routinely vaccinated against diseases such as tuberculosis, diphtheria and poliomyelitis. When people travel abroad, they often have vaccinations against diseases they may not encounter in their own country, such as malaria and yellow fever.

Safety

There are still a lot of arguments about the safety of some vaccinations. In recent years, a combined vaccine for mumps, measles and rubella has become available. Some doctors think that there might be a connection between this vaccine and certain conditions, including autism and some bowel diseases. Some parents are happy to have their children vaccinated, some choose not to vaccinate their children at all and others choose to have the three vaccines separately. There are arguments for and against each course of action.

How do vaccines work?

When you are vaccinated, you are injected with a small amount of dead or weakened **microbe** material. Your immune system responds to this as if it is real, live material. T-cells and B-cells become activated, **antibodies** are produced and a full specific immune response is launched. Memory cells remain afterwards and, as a result, if live microbes invade your body in the future, the memory cells are ready to mount a swift and strong response. This prevents you from suffering from the illness.

MONOCLONAL ANTIBODIES

Antibodies are **proteins** that are produced by B **lymphocytes** in response to specific **antigens**. Scientists have developed ways of producing large amounts of identical antibodies that can be used for a variety of purposes. These are called monoclonal antibodies.

Developing the technique

In 1975, two scientists, Georges Kohler and Cesar Milstein, produced the first monoclonal antibodies, and were awarded a Nobel Prize for their work. They injected an antigen into a mouse, and then removed activated lymphocytes from the mouse's **spleen**. In their laboratory, they fused an activated lymphocyte with a tumour cell, producing a new type of cell, called a hybridoma. This new cell divided again and again, producing a clone of identical cells. Each cell produced identical antibodies to the antigen they had originally injected into the mouse. Their technique gave them an unlimited supply of identical antibody molecules. Because all the antibodies come from one clone, they are called monoclonal antibodies.

This diagram shows the stages in the production of monoclonal antibodies:
1. Mouse injected with antigen.
2. Mouse's immune system is stimulated, and lymphocytes are actuated.
3. Active lymphocytes are collected and fused with tumour cell to make hybridoma.
4. Tumour cell is used because it is able to divide many times.
5. Hybridoma cells divide many times to make clones of identical cells.
6. Clone cells produce antibodies.
7. Monoclonal antibodies are isolated for cultivation.

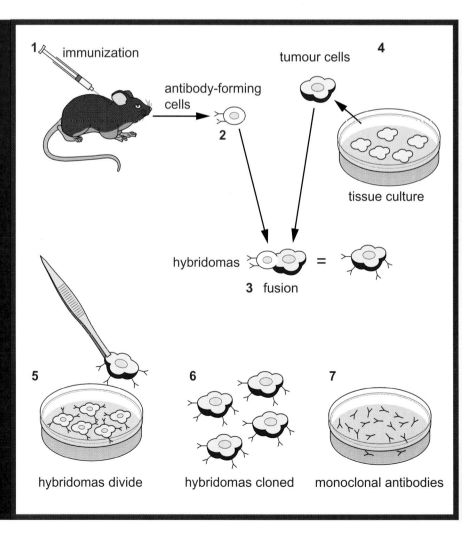

Monoclonal antibodies can be used for a variety of things, including:

- reducing **rejection** of tissue transplants
- treatment of some inflammatory diseases
- prevention of clogging of arteries in patients with heart disease.

Rejection of tissue transplants

The US government approved the use of a monoclonal antibody in kidney transplant patients in 1986. This antibody attacks the T-cells that cause tissue rejection. Doctors have found that patients given the monoclonal antibody are significantly less likely to reject the transplanted kidney than patients given more conventional drug treatments.

Other uses

Some other applications of monoclonal antibodies are in cancer treatment. Antibodies can be made specific to antigens found on the surface of cancer cells. If an anti-cancer drug is attached to the antibodies, they will deliver the drug straight to the cancer cells in the body without damage to any other cells and tissues. A radioactive tracer could also be linked to cancer-specific antibodies, and be used to find out the precise location of cancer cells in the body.

This scientist is isolating cells for use in monoclonal antibody production.

Problems

There are some problems in the production and use of monoclonal antibodies. The human immune system can recognize the mouse material within the monoclonal antibodies, and quickly mounts an immune response to destroy them. Also, people are increasingly uncomfortable with the use of animals in science, and without using mice we have no simple way of producing the initial active lymphocytes needed. It is possible to use humans instead, but few people would be happy with the idea of being used themselves.

ALLERGY

An **allergy** is sensitivity to something that most people do not react to. The substance that causes the allergy is called an allergen. Allergies to many everyday substances such as pollen, insect stings, animal fur and house dust mites are common. Some **allergic reactions** can be very quick, developing almost immediately, while other allergic reactions can take hours or days to develop.

Immediate allergic reaction

This type of reaction develops within minutes of exposure to the allergen. B-cells respond to the allergen by producing extra IgE **antibodies**. These bind to the surface of some white blood cells. The allergen particles bind to the IgE antibodies, and the white blood cells release **histamine** and other chemicals. These start off an **inflammatory response**, and may also cause muscle contractions in the airways and increased production of **mucus**. The person may suffer from inflammation, and may have difficulty breathing and a runny nose.

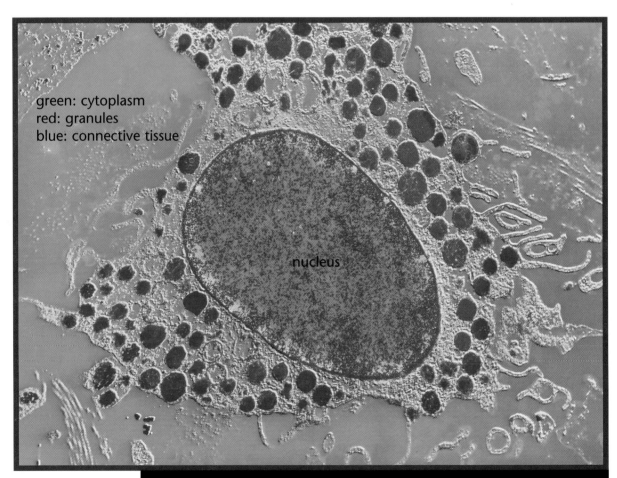

green: cytoplasm
red: granules
blue: connective tissue

nucleus

This photomicrograph shows a white blood cell with granules containing histamine, serotonin and herapin.

Anaphylactic shock

Severe allergic reactions are known as 'anaphylactic shock'. This is life-threatening, and must be treated as quickly as possible. People who know they are at risk from anaphylactic shock usually carry a small device, called an EpiPen, with them. This contains a simple mechanism that allows them to inject a dose of epinephrine (adrenaline) into a muscle. Epinephrine makes breathing easier and helps to control the heartbeat. A medi-bracelet is often worn, too, with details of the person's condition, so that other people know what treatment should be given.

Anaphylactic shock is not common, but some allergens are known to provoke very swift and severe reactions. Wasp and bee stings can provoke anaphylactic shock in sensitized people, and increasing numbers of people are experiencing severe allergic reactions to peanuts.

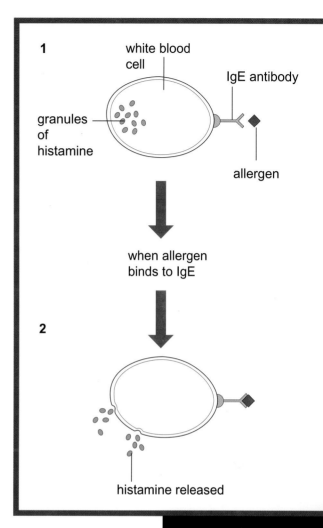

Delayed allergic reaction

In some cases, the allergic reaction does not appear until 12 to 72 hours after exposure to the allergen. This happens when the allergen travels to the **lymph nodes**. T-cells multiply, and some return to the place where the allergen first entered the body. There, they activate **macrophages**, and an inflammatory response begins.

BCG

The BCG blood test for immunity to tuberculosis uses this mechanism. A small amount of inactive TB material is pricked into the skin. After a couple of days, the skin is examined. If a red weal appears, it proves that the person is already sensitive to the tuberculosis **bacterium** and does not need to be vaccinated. If there is no red weal, the person is not sensitized to the bacterium, and vaccination will give them protection against the disease.

These diagrams show what happens in an immediate allergic reaction:
1. A white blood cell with an attached IgE antibody comes into contact with an allergen.
2. The allergen attaches to the antibody, and the white blood cell releases histamine.

COPING WITH ALLERGIES

People who suffer from allergies need to find a way of coping with their **allergy** so that it does not interfere with their life too much. Some allergies are easy to identify, and it may be easy to avoid contact with the allergen. Others are harder to identify, and the allergen may be difficult to avoid.

Airborne allergens

Many people suffer from hay fever. This is caused by an **allergic reaction** to pollen (usually from grass) in the air. In most cases, it lasts for just a short time while grass pollen is released. It may be prolonged if the person is allergic to more than one type of pollen. Hay fever involves red, itchy eyes, a runny nose and excessive sneezing. Weather forecasts now often give a 'pollen index' during the height of the hay fever period, in May and June. If you suffer from hay fever, it is a good idea to avoid being outside too much when there is a lot of pollen in the air. Some drugs, including anti-histamines, are available to combat hay fever.

Hay fever causes red, itchy eyes and a runny nose.

Food allergies

Allergies to foods can produce a wide variety of symptoms, but there is usually a feeling of sickness, followed by vomiting and diarrhoea, within hours of eating the food. In severe cases, the lips and tongue may become red and swollen. A skin rash may also appear hours or days later.

Identifying the substance to which a person is allergic is sometimes very simple. For example, if you know that you always feel sick after eating shellfish, the answer is simple: don't eat shellfish!

Allergens via the skin

Touching something to which you are allergic will cause an **inflammatory response**. Common allergens are wool, some metals, some plants, sticking plasters and chemicals in some soap powders. Many adults suffer from dermatitis, and eczema in children is often caused by allergies. The best way of dealing with this type of allergy is to avoid all contact with the allergen, if possible. Creams and ointments can often help to make the dry, cracked skin of eczema more bearable.

Testing for allergies

Identifying allergies is not always straightforward, especially if several different allergens are involved. Doctors may carry out skin tests by putting a tiny drop of liquid containing an allergen onto the skin, and pricking it into the skin with a fine needle. If the person is allergic to the allergen, a red weal appears on the skin after a few minutes. Many different allergens can be tested at the same time, each at a different place on the skin.

Skin tests can be used to help to identify the cause of an allergy.

Food allergies can often be identified by using an elimination diet. The patient is allowed to eat a very simple diet of water, one type of meat and one vegetable for a few days. Other foods are introduced one at a time. If the patient feels better, the allergen has been excluded. If they begin to feel ill again, it must be due to one of the foods added back into their diet. It is important that elimination diets are carried out under the supervision of a doctor, so that the patient can be properly monitored.

AUTOIMMUNITY

Autoimmunity is the name given to any condition where a person's immune system begins to attack his or her own body.

In most people, the immune system only responds to foreign ('non-self') **antigens**. It recognizes the body's own antigens as 'self' and ignores them. If this goes wrong, the immune system begins to recognize the body's own tissues as 'non-self', and mounts an immune response against them.

Recognizing 'self'

While T **lymphocytes** (T-cells) are maturing in the **thymus** gland, they go through a selection process. Those that recognize body tissues as 'self' and do not react will survive. Any that do not recognize 'self' will die. Any that recognize 'self' and react will also die. A similar process of selection of B-cells occurs as they develop in the **bone marrow**.

There are two main causes of autoimmunity:

- If part of the body becomes damaged in some way, antigens that would normally remain hidden may become exposed to the immune system. Because the immune system has not met them before, it cannot recognize them as 'self', and so it begins to attack them. An example of this happening is a condition called *sympathetic ophthalmia*. In this condition, one eye becomes damaged and new antigens are exposed. The immune system attacks these antigens – and the other, healthy eye, too.
- A random genetic change in a B-cell or T-cell may give rise to a clone of lymphocytes that react against the body's own tissue.

This shows an X-ray of the hand of a rheumatoid arthritis sufferer. You can see how the joints are deformed.

Several disease conditions are the result of autoimmunity. These include:

Rheumatoid arthritis

In this disease, some B-cells change to produce a different form of IgM **antibody**, called rheumatoid factor. This reacts against normal IgG, and causes inflammation of joints. The joints become swollen and painful, eventually becoming deformed and stiff. Treatment with painkillers helps the patient to cope, and a range of drugs, including **steroids**, can often keep the disease under control and prevent some of its crippling effects.

Multiple sclerosis

In this disease, the **protein** coverings of nerves become inflamed, damaged and scarred, as a result of action by the body's own immune system. The affected nerves cannot transmit signals to and from the brain properly, and the person's movements are gradually restricted. Although there is some evidence for a **genetic** link, scientists have not proved that it is an inherited condition. A drug, called beta interferon, can slow the progress of the disease in some cases, but it is an expensive treatment, and not all patients are able to tolerate the powerful drug. Cannabis is reported to help alleviate pain in many sufferers, but there is a problem, because cannabis is still an illegal substance in some countries.

The famous cellist Jacqueline du Pré suffered from multiple sclerosis.

IMMUNODEFICIENCY AND IMMUNOSUPPRESSION

If a person is suffering from an **immunodeficiency** or **immunosuppression**, their immune system is unable to respond effectively to **antigens**. This means that they are vulnerable to infections and have no way of overcoming them.

Immunodeficiency

Some people are born with an immune system that cannot function properly. They may have no T-cells, or no B-cells. If they have B-cells, they may not be able to produce a full range of **antibodies**.

IgA deficiency

Selective IgA deficiency is a condition where a person cannot produce IgA antibodies. It is important that the body is protected at surfaces that come into contact with the world around it, such as the mouth and nose, the lungs, the throat, the digestive tract and the eyes. It is mainly IgA that protects these surfaces from infection. People with IgA deficiency, therefore, often suffer from recurrent infections, such as ear infections, sinusitis and pneumonia, and they may have to remain on **antibiotics** for longer than usual.

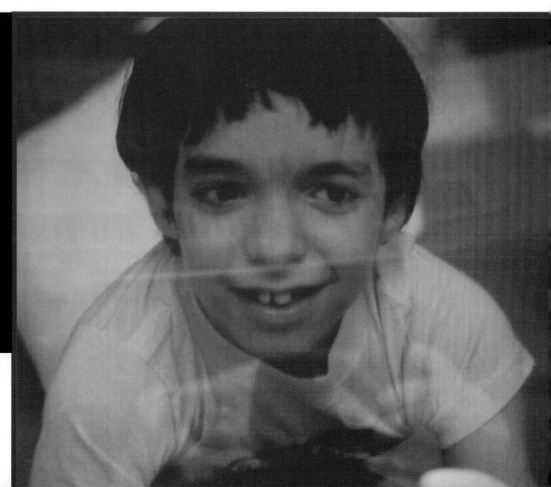

This boy was born with SCID. He has no resistance to any infection. He must live enclosed in a sterile plastic bubble until doctors can find a way to get his immune system functioning properly.

Severe combined immunodeficiency syndrome (SCID)

Severe combined immunodeficiency syndrome (SCID) is a very serious, though fortunately rare, inherited condition. Babies born with SCID have no B-cells and no T-cells. As a result, they have practically no defence against any infection. They often die in early childhood, but **bone marrow** transplants have been found to help some children with SCID.

Immunosuppression

Sometimes, a person's immune system needs to be switched off, or suppressed. Drugs that can do this are called 'immunosuppressants'. They play an important part in helping a patient's body to accept a tissue transplant, preventing the patient's immune system from recognizing the transplant as 'non-self' and attacking it.

Immunosuppressant drugs have to be used very carefully, however. By switching off a patient's immune system, the drugs remove the patient's ability to react to an infection. Also, any abnormal cells, such as cancer cells, will not be detected by the immune system while it is switched off and, therefore, will not be killed.

As people age

Other conditions, such as viral infections, can lead to a reduction in the efficiency of the immune system. As people age, their immune systems slowly become less efficient. T-cells become less responsive to antigens, fewer T-cells respond to infections and B-cells produce fewer antibodies. Together, these changes mean that a person becomes more likely to suffer from infections as they get older.

The fungus *Tolypocladium inflatum* produces the immunosuppressant drug cyclosporin.

AIDS stands for Acquired Immune Deficiency Syndrome, and is caused by infection with HIV (human **immunodeficiency virus**). Many people with HIV infection do not have AIDS, and may show no signs of illness for many years.

There are many myths about HIV and AIDS, and people often feel that they do not want to mix with anyone that might have the disease. However, there is really no basis for such ideas, because HIV cannot be passed from one person to another by casual contact. The virus is fragile and can only survive outside the body for a short time. It can be killed by disinfectants, and by normal washing of dishes and clothes. HIV can only be passed from one person to another by mixing body fluids, by sexual contact or by sharing needles between drug users. Some **haemophiliacs** have been infected with HIV after receiving contaminated blood products, but all blood donations are now screened for HIV in an attempt to prevent this happening in the future.

This photomicrograph shows HIV particles being released from T lymphocytes into the bloodstream.

What is HIV?

HIV is a single strand of **genetic** material surrounded by a **protein** coat. It enters a **host cell**, and uses parts of the host cell to make copies of its genetic material and to assemble new protein coats. The new viruses that have been made then leave the host cell and circulate in the blood to infect other host cells. This process is the same as that used by other viruses. HIV is different because the host cells it targets are **T lymphocytes**. As the number of virus particles in the body increases, the number of T-cells slowly decreases and the person's immune system becomes less efficient.

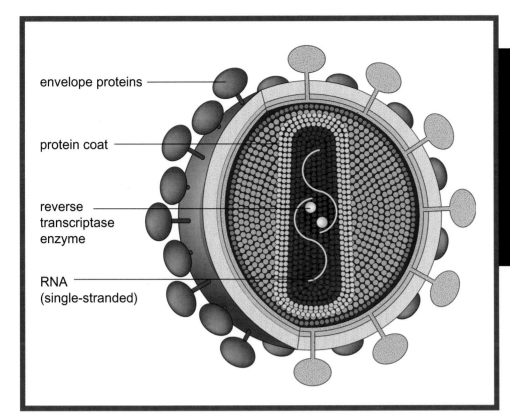

envelope proteins

protein coat

reverse transcriptase enzyme

RNA (single-stranded)

HIV viruses are so small that hundreds of thousands could fit on the head of a pin!

HIV positive

People with HIV infection are said to be HIV positive. This means that a blood test has shown there are **antibodies** to the HIV virus circulating in the person's blood. Some people with HIV infection may have no symptoms at all. Others suffer from an illness like flu, with joint pain, a sore throat and swollen **lymph nodes**. It can take several years for HIV to destroy enough T-cells to make the person immunodeficient but, finally, the immune system collapses. The person suffers from one infection after another. Eventually, many AIDS sufferers die from a common infection that their bodies cannot fight.

Treatment

AIDS cannot be cured at present, and no vaccine is available. However, there are two groups of drugs that can help to keep HIV-infected people well:

- drugs that interfere with the reproduction of the virus genetic material
- drugs that interfere with the production of the protein coats.

Most people with HIV benefit from a 'triple therapy', consisting of two drugs to block genetic material reproduction and one drug to block protein coat production. This treatment leads to a reduction in the number of virus particles and an increase in the number of healthy T-cells. The triple therapy also seems to delay the progress from HIV to AIDS. The drugs involved are extremely expensive, however, and many people cannot tolerate the harsh side effects that they produce.

damaged or diseased, a patient faced certain death. Nowadays, in many cases, advances in transplant techniques allow doctors to replace the failing organ with a healthy one donated from another person. This gives the patient the chance of a new life.

Transplants are needed to provide a patient with a new organ or tissue to replace their own, which is damaged or diseased. The organs most commonly transplanted are hearts, lungs, livers and kidneys. Donated organs may come from people who have died, in a traffic accident, for example, or, in the case of kidneys, from a close family member, who may donate one of their own kidneys to save a relative. **Bone marrow** transplants within families are also common.

A patient's body can reject transplanted organs. This means that the immune system of the person receiving the organ (the host) recognizes **antigens** on the surface of the transplanted organ as 'non-self', and reacts against it.

Tissue type

Every person has a set of antigens on every cell of their body, determined by their **genetic** material. There are many different possible antigens, and they can be found together in an almost infinite variety of combinations. Your own personal set of antigens is called your '**tissue type**'.

The risk of **rejection** is reduced if the tissue type of the transplanted organ is similar to that of the host. Ideally, the tissue types of transplant and host would be identical, but this is rarely ever possible. Before a transplant is performed, scientists carry out 'tissue-typing' tests to check that the transplant and host are not too different.

National and international databanks

This scientist is testing the tissue type of a patient.

exist, keeping records of tissue types of patients and potential donors. This means that, when a donor organ becomes available, it can quickly be matched with a suitable patient.

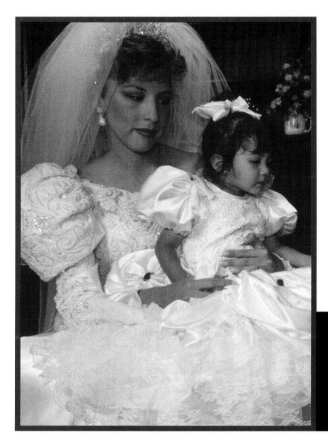

This girl has had a successful bone marrow transplant to cure her leukaemia. Bone marrow was donated by her younger sister.

Stem cell transplants

Stem cells can be transplanted instead of bone marrow. Stem cells are the cells from which all blood cells develop. Some stem cells circulate in the blood and can be collected by a process called 'apheresis'. Stem cell transplants can be from a donor, or a patient's own healthy stem cells can be collected and stored before radiotherapy or chemotherapy treatment begins. When the treatment is completed, their own stem cells can be transplanted back to restore normal bone marrow function.

Suitable donors

Family members often have very similar tissue types and can, therefore, often provide tissue for transplantation. Bone marrow transplants between brother and sister, or parent and child, are common, and are often successful in treating diseases such as leukaemia.

To reduce the risk of a transplant being rejected, the patient is usually given **immunosuppressant** drugs. These 'switch off' the immune system so that it cannot attack the transplant.

In some cases of bone marrow transplant, the opposite to transplant rejection can occur. **Lymphocytes** from the transplanted bone marrow recognize the host's body as 'non-self' and begin to attack it. This is called a graft-versus-host reaction (GVH). It can be treated with **steroids** or immunosuppressant drugs.

OTHER IMMUNE SYSTEM PROBLEMS

Infectious mononucleosis

This illness is often known as glandular fever. It is caused by the Epstein-Barr **virus**, and is most common in teenagers and young adults. Girls are three times more likely to suffer from it than boys.

The virus particles multiply in B **lymphocytes** in lymphatic tissue, and spread into the bloodstream. The infection usually causes a fever, tiredness, a sore throat and a headache. The **lymph nodes** in the neck are often swollen, and there may be liver problems. Blood tests show a very high number of lymphocytes in the blood. There is no cure for the illness, but it usually lasts just a few weeks and does not have long-term effects.

In adults, the virus cannot be passed from one person to another by casual contact. In children and teenagers, it can be passed during close contact, such as by kissing and sharing drinking glasses.

Myalgic encephalomyelitis (ME)

This illness has different names in different places. In Japan, it is known as 'low natural killer cell syndrome' and in the UK it is called

'myalgic encephalomyelitis' (usually shortened to ME) or 'post-viral syndrome'. In the USA, it is referred to as 'yuppie flu' and 'chronic fatigue immune dysfunction syndrome' (CFIDS).

Symptoms

People with ME have flu-like symptoms and suffer from extreme tiredness. There are often other symptoms such as hair loss, joint and muscle pain, depression and insomnia. The illness may last for several months, after which the person is fully well again. Some people find they have a recurrence after a few years. In other people, the illness lasts for many years without significant improvement.

This electronmicrograph shows Epstein-Barr viruses, responsible for infectious mononucleosis.

Causes

The exact cause of ME is unknown. Scientists think that it may be linked to a viral infection, but there also seem to be some **genetic** factors making some people more susceptible to it than others. Extreme stress is thought to play a part in the development of the illness, and there may be some dietary links.

The illness initially weakens the patient's immune system, allowing infections to develop. Some T-cells seem to respond by overreacting, while others under-react. There is no cure for ME at present, but many patients do improve after a period of resting and avoiding unnecessary stress.

Malignant diseases

Cells of the lymphatic system and immune system can undergo changes that transform them from normal cells into cancer cells.

Lymphomas are cancers of the lymphatic system. Hodgkin's Disease is a lymphoma that most commonly affects teenagers and young adults. It begins in lymphoid tissue, often in the lymph nodes of the neck. These swell, and other lymph nodes become involved. The cause of Hodgkin's Disease is unknown, but it is usually completely curable by a combination of radiotherapy and chemotherapy.

Hodgkin's Disease can occur in both adults and children, and about 10–15% of all cases occur in children under 16 years old.

Leukaemia

Leukaemias are cancers of the blood and can arise in **bone marrow** or lymphatic tissue. There are several different forms of leukaemia, but they are all caused by white blood cells failing to mature properly. These abnormal cells cannot fight infections. So many of them are produced that they eventually clog up the system, preventing the production of normal blood cells. Many leukaemias are curable with radiotherapy, chemotherapy and bone marrow transplants.

WHAT CAN GO WRONG WITH MY IMMUNE SYSTEM?

This book has explained the different parts of the immune system, why they are important, and how they can be damaged by injury and illness. This table summarizes some of the problems that can affect the immune system. It also gives information about how each problem can be treated.

Many of the problems below can be avoided or prevented by maintaining a healthy lifestyle. Taking regular exercise and getting plenty of rest are important, as is eating a balanced diet. This is especially important in your teenage years, when your body is still developing. The table tells you some of the ways you can prevent injury and illness.

Remember, if you think something is wrong with your body, you should always talk to a trained medical professional, such as a doctor or a school nurse. Regular medical check-ups are an important part of maintaining a healthy body.

Illness or injury	Cause	Symptoms	Prevention	Treatment
allergic reaction	exposure to something to which the immune system has become hypersensitive	various, including skin rash, sickness, diarrhoea, breathing difficulty and a runny nose	avoid exposure to the triggering substance	depends on the cause, but antihistamines may help in many cases
myalgic encephalomyelitis (ME)	unknown, but maybe linked to stress, diet and viral infection	extreme tiredness, flu-like symptoms, depression, joint and muscle pains	maintain a healthy lifestyle, with a balanced diet, and avoid stress where possible	no cure yet, but rest, reduction of stress and a restricted diet can help in many cases
infectious mononucleosis (glandular fever)	infection by Epstein-Barr **virus**	fever, tiredness, sore throat, headache and swollen **lymph nodes**	avoid infection by the virus, for example, by not sharing drinking glasses	no cure, but with rest, recovery is usually within a few weeks
tonsilitis	infection of tonsils, usually by **bacteria**, sometimes by a virus	sore throat, difficulty swallowing, earache, high temperature and swollen nodes	maintain a healthy lifestyle, with a balanced diet and a good standard of hygiene	**antibiotics** to combat bacterial infection; in severe cases, tonsils may be removed surgically

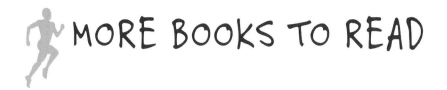

MORE BOOKS TO READ

101 Questions About Your Immune System You Felt Defenseless to Answer...Until Now, Faith Hickman Brynie (Twenty First Century Books, 2000)

Discovery: Inside AIDS: HIV Attacks the Immune System, Conrad J. Storad (Lerner Publications, 1998)

21st Century Health and Wellness: The Immune System, Edward Edelson (Chelsea House Publications, 1999)

The Smallpox Slayer, Alan Brown (Hodder Wayland, 2001)

The Blue Death, Judy Allen (Hodder Wayland, 2001)

The Usborne Internet Linked Library of Science: Human Body, K. Rogers (Usborne, 2001)

How It Works: Funny Bones, Anita Ganeri (Heinemann Library, 1997)

How It Works: Creature Features, Anita Ganeri (Heinemann Library, 1997)

GLOSSARY

allergy sensitivity to something that other people do not react to

allergic reaction reaction by the body to an antigen to which it is sensitive, such as the runny nose and sore eyes of hay fever sufferers when exposed to pollens

antibiotics drugs used to fight infections. They destroy micro-organisms such as bacteria or fungi, but are not effective against viruses.

antibody chemical made by lymphocytes that binds to a specific antigen

antigen chemical or organism that stimulates an allergic response

antigen substance that provokes a response by the immune system

anaphylactic shock acute response to an antigen that must be treated as an emergency

autoimmunity condition where the immune system recognizes part of the body as 'non-self', and begins to attack it

bacteria microbes that can be useful or can cause disease

bone marrow part of the bone where white blood cells are produced

cytoplasm part of a cell outside the nucleus but inside the cell membrane

enzyme protein that acts as a catalyst in chemical reactions

genetic to do with passing characteristics from one generation to the next

haemophiliac person suffering from haemophilia, a hereditary condition in which blood does not clot properly

histamine chemical released when tissue is damaged

host cell cell in which a virus makes more copies of itself

immunodeficiency condition where some or all components of the immune system are missing

immunosuppression condition where the immune system is unable to operate efficiently

inflammatory response non-specific response to an antigen

intestines part of the digestive system

lymph clear, colourless liquid that flows through the lymphatic system

lymphatic system system of drainage vessels, also involved in the body's immune responses

lymph node swelling on a lymph duct, where some white blood cells are made and some immune responses take place

lymphocyte white blood cell that is involved in specific responses to antigens

macrophage specialized phagocyte that engulfs and destroys foreign material

membrane thin covering layer of tissue

microbe living organism, such as a bacterium, that can only be seen with a microscope

micro-organism tiny living thing that can only be seen under a microscope

mucus sticky, slimy fluid that provides lubrication inside many organs and vessels

neutrophil specialized phagocyte

phagocyte white blood cell that engulfs microbes and cell debris

phagocytosis process of engulfing and destroying microbes and cell debris

platelets particles involved in blood clotting

protein complex chemical that is a component of many of the body's structures

rejection process by which transplanted tissue is recognized as 'non-self', and attacked by the immune system

spleen largest organ in the lymphatic system

stem cells cells from which all white blood cells develop

steroids human-made drugs that are similar to some chemicals found naturally in the body

thymus part of the lymphatic system where T lymphocytes mature

tissue type set of antigens on the surface of the body's cells

vaccination protection against a disease by injection of dead or weakened antigen

virus microbe that uses the body's own cells to make copies of itself

The lymphatic system.

INDEX